THE BOOK OF MEN

THE BOOK OF MEN

Poems

Dorianne Laux

W. W. NORTON & COMPANY

New York · London

Copyright © 2011 by Dorianne Laux

For information about permission to reproduce selections from this book, write to Permissions, W. W. Norton & Company, Inc., 500 Fifth Avenue, New York, NY 10110

For information about special discounts for bulk purchases, please contact W. W. Norton Special Sales at specialsales@wwnorton.com or 800-233-4830

Manufacturing by Courier Westford
Book design by JAMdesign
Production manager: Julia Druskin

Library of Congress Cataloging-in-Publication Data

Laux, Dorianne.
The book of men : poems / Dorianne Laux. — 1st ed.
p. cm.
ISBN 978-0-393-07955-5 (hardcover)
I. Title.
PS3562.A8455B66 2011
811'.54—dc22

2010037722

W. W. Norton & Company, Inc.
500 Fifth Avenue, New York, N.Y. 10110
www.wwnorton.com

W. W. Norton & Company Ltd.
Castle House, 75/76 Wells Street, London W1T 3QT

1 2 3 4 5 6 7 8 9 0

for Philip Levine

To pass among them, or touch any one,

or rest my arm ever so lightly round his or her neck

for a moment—what is this, then?

—WALT WHITMAN

CONTENTS

ONE

TWO

THE BOOK OF MEN

ONE

STAFF SGT. METZ

Metz is alive for now, standing in line
at the airport Starbucks in his camo gear
and buzz cut, his beautiful new
camel-colored suede boots. His hands
are thick-veined. The good blood
still flows through, given an extra surge
when he slurps his latte, a fleck of foam
caught on his bottom lip.

I can see into the canal in his right ear,
a narrow darkness spiraling deep inside his head
toward the place of dreaming and fractions,
ponds of quiet thought.

In the sixties my brother left for Vietnam,
a war no one understood, and I hated him for it.
When my boyfriend was drafted I made a vow
to write a letter every day, and then broke it.
I was a girl torn between love and the idea of love.
I burned their letters in the metal trash bin
behind the broken fence. It was the summer of love
and I wore nothing under my cotton vest,
my Mexican skirt.

I see Metz later, outside baggage claim,
hunched over a cigarette, mumbling
into his cell phone. He's more real to me now
than my brother was to me then, his big eyes
darting from car to car as they pass.
I watch him breathe into his hands.

I don't believe in anything anymore:
god, country, money or love.
All that matters to me now
is his life, the body so perfectly made,
mysterious in its workings, its oiled
and moving parts, the whole of him
standing up and raising one arm
to hail a bus, his legs pulling him forward,
all muscle and sinew and living gristle,
the countless bones of his foot trapped in his boot,
stepping off the red curb.

A SHORT HISTORY OF THE APPLE

> The crunch is the thing, a certain joy in crashing through
> living tissue, a memory of Neanderthal days.
>
> —EDWARD BUNYARD, *The Anatomy of Dessert*, 1929

Teeth at the skin. Anticipation.
Then flesh. Grain on the tongue.
Eve's knees ground in the dirt
of paradise. Newton watching
gravity happen. The history
of apples in each starry core,
every papery chamber's bright
bitter seed. Woody stem
an infant tree. William Tell
and his lucky arrow. Orchards
of the Fertile Crescent. Bushels.
Fire blight. Scab and powdery mildew.
Cedar apple rust. The apple endures.
Born of the wild rose, of crab ancestors.
The first pip raised in Kazakhstan.
Snow White with poison on her lips.
The buried blades of Halloween.
Budding and grafting. John Chapman
in his tin pot hat. Oh Westward
Expansion. Apple pie. American
as. Hard cider. Winter banana.
Melt-in-the-mouth made sweet
by hives of Britain's honeybees:
white man's flies. O eat. O eat.

BAKERSFIELD, 1969

I used to visit a boy in Bakersfield, hitchhike
to the San Diego terminal and ride the bus for hours
through the sun-blasted San Fernando Valley
just to sit on his fold-down bed in a trailer
parked in the side yard of his parents' house,
drinking Southern Comfort from a plastic cup.
His brother was a sessions man for Taj Mahal,
and he played guitar, too, picked at it like a scab.
Once his mother knocked on the tin door
to ask us in for dinner. She watched me
from the sides of her eyes while I ate.
When I offered to wash the dishes she told me
she wouldn't stand her son being taken
advantage of. I said I had no intention
of taking anything and set the last dish
carefully in the rack. He was a bit slow,
like he'd been hit hard on the back of the head,
but nothing dramatic. We didn't talk much anyway,
just drank and smoked and fucked and slept
through the ferocious heat. I found a photograph
he took of me getting back on the bus or maybe
stepping off into his arms. I'm wearing jeans
with studs punched into the cuffs,
a T-shirt with stars on the sleeves, a pair

of stolen bowling shoes and a purse I made
while I was in the loony bin, wobbly X's
embroidered on burlap with gaudy orange yarn.
I don't remember how we met. When I look
at this picture I think I might not even
remember this boy if he hadn't taken it
and given it to me, written his name under mine
on the back. I stopped seeing him
after that thing with his mother. I didn't know
I didn't know anything yet. I liked him.
That's what I remember. That,
and the I-don't-know-what degree heat
that rubbed up against the trailer's metal sides,
steamed in through the cracks between the door
and porthole windows, pressed down on us
from the ceiling and seeped through the floor,
crushing us into the damp sheets. How we endured it,
sweat streaming down our naked bodies, the air
sucked from our lungs as we slept. Taj Mahal says
If you ain't scared, you ain't right. Back then
I was scared most of the time. But I acted
tough, like I knew every street.
What I liked about him was that he wasn't acting.
Even his sweat tasted sweet.

LATE-NIGHT TV

Again the insomnia of August,
a night sky buffed by the heat,
the air so still a ringing phone
three blocks away sings
through the fan's slow moving blades.
The sleeping cat at the foot of the bed
twitches in a pool of dusty sheets,
her fur malt-colored, electric.

Time to rub the shoulder's tight knots out
with a thumb, flip on the TV, watch a man
douse a white blouse with ink before dipping
that sad sleeve into a clear bucket.

What cup of love poured him into this world?
Did his mother touch her lips
to his womb-battered crown
and inhale his scent?
Did his new father lift him and name him?
He was fed, clothed, taught to talk.
Someone must have picked him up
each time he wobbled and fell.
There might have been a desk, a history book,
pencils in a box, a succession
of wheeled toys.

By what back road did he travel
to this late-night station?
By what imperceptible set of circumstances
does he arrive in my bedroom on a summer night,
pinching a shirt collar between his fingers,
his own invention locked in a blue box,
a rainbow slashed across it?

Somewhere in the universe is a palace
where each of us is imprinted with a map,
the one path seared into the circuits of our brains.
It signals us to turn left at the green light,
right at the dead tree.

We know nothing of how it all works,
how we end up in one bed or another,
speak one language instead of the others,
what heat draws us to our life's work
or keeps us from a dream until it's nothing
but a blister we scratch in our sleep.

His voice is soothing, his teeth crooked,
his arms strong and smooth below rolled-up cuffs.
I have the power to make him disappear
with one touch, though if I do the darkness
will swallow me, drown me.

Time to settle back against the pillows
and gaze deeply into the excitement
welling in his eyes. *It's a miracle,* he whispers
as the burnt moon slips across the sky.
Then he dumps the grainy crystals in
and stirs the water with a wooden spoon.

MICK JAGGER (WORLD TOUR, 2008)

He stands on stage
after spot-lit stage, yowling
with his rubber mouth. If you
turn off the sound he's
a ruminating bovine,
a baby's face tasting his first
sour orange or spitting
spooned oatmeal out.
Rugose cheeks and beef
jerky jowls, shrubby hair
waxed, roughed up, arms
slung dome-ward, twisted
branches of a tough tree, knees
stomping high as his sunken chest.
Oddities aside, he's a hybrid
of stamina and slouch,
tummy pooch, pouches under
his famous invasive rolling eyes.
He flutters like the pages
of a dirty book, doing
the sombrero dance, rocking
the microphone's
round black foot, one hand

gripping the skinny metal rod,
the other pumping its victory fist
like he's flushing a chain toilet.
Old as the moon and sleek
as a puma circling the herd.
The vein in his forehead
pops. His hands drop into fists.
He bows like a beggar then rises
like a monarch. Sir Mick,
our bony ruler. Jagger, slumping
offstage shining with sweat.
Oh please don't die. Not now,
not ever, not yet.

JUNEAU

In Alaska I slept in a bed on stilts, one arm
pressed against the ice-feathered window,
the heat on high, sweat darkening the collar
of my cotton thermals. I worked hard to buy that bed,
hiked toward it when the men in the booths
were finished crushing hundred-dollar bills
into my hand, pitchers of beer balanced on my shoulder
set down like pots of gold. My shift ended at 5 AM:
station tables wiped clean, salt and peppers
replenished, ketchups married. I walked the dirt road
in my stained apron and snow boots, wool scarf,
second-hand gloves, steam rising
off the backs of horses wading chest deep in fog.
I walked home slow under Orion, his starry belt
heavy beneath the cold carved moon.
My room was still, quiet, squares of starlight
set down like blank pages on the yellow quilt.
I left the heat on because I could afford it, the house
hot as a sauna, and shed my sweater and skirt,
toed off my boots, slung my damp socks
over the oil heater's coils. I don't know now
why I ever left. I slept like the dead
while outside my window the sun rose
low over the glacier, and the glacier did its best

to hold on, though one morning I woke to hear it
giving up, sloughing off a chunk of antediluvian ice,
a sound like an iron door opening on a bent hinge.
Those undefined days I stared into the blue scar
where the ice face had been, so clear and crystalline
it hurt. I slept in my small room and all night—
or what passed for night that far north—
the geography of the world outside my window
was breaking and falling and changing shape.
And I woke to it and looked at it and didn't speak.

LEARNING TO DRIVE

The long miles down the back road
I learned to drive on. The boy riding
shotgun. His hand on my hand on

the gear shift knob, our eyes locked
on the dusty windshield, the cracked
asphalt, old airstrip, the nothing spreading

for miles: scrub brush, heat waves, sky,
a few thin contrails. His patience
endless. My clumsiness: the grinding

gears, the fumbled clutch. The wrench
of it popped like an arm from its socket,
his blue, beloved '57 Ford lurching,

stalled in the dirt. I was 16, he was older,
his football-player shoulders muscular,
wide. Where did he get his kindness?

Why spend it on a girl like me: skinny,
serious, her nails bitten, her legs
bruised. Hours under summer's

relentless heat, his car stumbling
across the barren lot until I got it,
understood how to lift my left foot,

press my right hand, in tandem, like dancing,
which I never learned to do, never wanted
to turn circles on the polished floor

of a dark auditorium, the bleachers
hemming me in. I drove toward the horizon,
gravel jitterbugging under his tires. Lizards

skittering. Jays rising to the buzz
of telephone wires. He taught me
how to handle a car, how to downshift

into second, peel out from a dead stop.
His fist hung from the open window,
knuckles clamped on a lit cigarette,

dragging smoke. We couldn't guess
where we were going. He didn't know
he was flying to Vietnam

and I was learning how to get out of there,
The Byrds singing "Eight Miles High"
when he turned up the radio

and told me to brake, opened his door,
slid out and stood on the desert road
to let me go it alone. His back pressed

against all that emptiness.

LIGHTER

Aim above morality.

—RUTH GORDON, *Harold and Maude*

Steal something worthless, something small,
every once in a while. A lighter from the counter
at the 7-Eleven. Hold that darkness in your hand.
Look straight into the eyes of the clerk
as you slip it in your pocket, her blue
bruised eyes. Don't justify it. Just take
your change, your cigarettes, and walk
out the door into the snow or hard rain,
sunlight bearing down, like a truck, on your back.
Call it luck when you don't get caught.
Breathe easy as you stand on the corner,
waiting, like everyone else, for the light to change,
following the cop car with your eyes
as it slowly rolls by, ignoring the baby
in its shaded stroller. Don't you want
something for nothing? Haven't you suffered?
Haven't you been beaten down, condemned
like a tenement, gone to bed hungry, alone?
Sit on a stone bench and dig deep for it,
touch your thumb to the greased metal wheel.
Call it a gift from the gods of fire.
Call it your due.

SUPERMAN

Superman sits on a tall building
smoking pot, holding the white plumes in,
palliative for the cancerous green glow
spreading its tentacles beneath his
blue uniform, his paraffin skin.

The pot also calms him so he can look
down through the leafy crowns of the Trees
of Heaven to patches of black asphalt
where a small dog chained to a grate
raises his leg against a sapling.

It's 2010 and the doctors have given him
another year in Metropolis. Another year
in paradise when he's high, another year
in hell when he's not.
A magazine falls from his lap. Lois
on the cover of *Fortune*, the planets
aligned behind her, starlight glancing off
her steely upswept hair.

He lifts his head from his hands
as the sun sets, the sound of muffled gunfire
in every city of the world ricochets
through his gray brain. He'll take care of it
tomorrow, the thankless, endless task
of catching dirty bombs and bullets,
though like the dishes piling up in the sink
there are always more.

365 dark days left to try to gather them all,
tunnel through to the earth's core
and bury them there. But for now he leans
his wide back against the stove-hot bricks
and stretches each long blue leg.
Blissfully stoned he doesn't notice
when his heel clips the chipped wing
of a granite angel, can't feel the Kryptonite
bending its rays up toward his scarlet heart.

MONKS IN THE GRANDE CHARTREUSE

Silent—the best are silent now.

—MATTHEW ARNOLD,

"Stanzas from the Grande Chartreuse"

Look down the long hall. Light
floods the cracks: a loaf of bread
hollowed out, kiln-fire gold.
They file by in white robes, winter
opening outside the curved windows,
snow folded like dough
over the vegetable gardens, clouds
low hammocks slung between frozen trees.
At work in the kitchen, the barn,
the sewing room, when the bells ring
they kneel where they are and pray.
In the library of gilt-edged books,
in their cells, they kneel. Alcoves
set with votives, kernels of yellow fire
struggling behind red glass, a table,
rough-hewn, piled with stiff linen.
Still water in stone carved basins,
touched with two fingers, shimmers.
A cat winds by like wind. They pray.
And when they rise to sing no one
hears them in their limestone valley.
The stars arch as night's back

lifts and bristles. They chant
with closed eyes. They eat soup,
grainy potato. Celery, pale, stringy,
floats. Carrots and beans sunk
to the bottom of the bowl. The heavy
brown bread, almost inedible, soaks.
Nothing enters or leaves this quiet.
No bird. No squirrel. Cold white,
every branch still.

MEN

It's tough being a guy, having to be gruff
and buff, the strong silent type, having to laugh
it off—pain, loss, sorrow, betrayal—or leave in a huff
and say *No big deal*, take a ride, listen to enough
loud rock and roll that it scours out your head, if
not your heart. Or to be called a fag or a poof
when you love something or someone, scuffing
a shoe across the floor, hiding a smile in a muffler
pulled up nose high, an eyebrow raised for the word quaff
used in casual conversation—wine, air, oil change at the Jiffy
Lube—gulping it down, a joke no one gets. It's rough,
yes, the tie around the neck, the starched white cuffs
too long, too short, frayed, frilled, rolled up. The self
isn't an easy quest for a beast with balls, a cock, proof
of something difficult to define or defend. Chief or chef,
thief or roofer, serf or sheriff, feet on the earth or aloof.
Son, brother, husband, lover, father, they are different
from us, except when they fall or stand alone on a wharf.

HOMICIDE DETECTIVE: A FILM NOIR

Smell of diesel fuel and dead trees
on a flatbed soaked to the bone.
Smell of dusty heater coils.
We got homicides in motels and apartments
all across the city: under the beds,
behind the doors, in the bathtubs.
It's where I come in at 5 AM,
paper cup of coffee dripping
down my sleeve, powdered
half-moon donut in my mouth.
Blood everywhere. Bodies
belly down, bodies faceup
on the kitchenette floor.
¿Dónde está? Que sera.
We got loose ends, we got
dead ends, we got split ends,
hair in the drains, fingerprints
on glass. This is where I stand,
my hat glittery with rain,
casting my restless shadow.

These are the dark hours,
dark times are these, hours
when the clock chimes once

as if done with it, tired of it: the sun,
the highways, the damnable
flowers strewn on the fake wool rug.

These are the flayed heart's flowers,
oil-black dahlias big as fists,
stems thick as wrists, striped, torn,
floating in the syrupy left-on music
but the bright world is done and I'm
a ghost touching the hair of the dead
with a gloved hand.

These are the done-for, the poor,
the defenseless, mostly women,
felled trees, limbs lashing
up into air, into rain,
as if time were nothing, hours,
clocks, highways, faces, don't step
on the petals, the upturned hands, stay
behind the yellow tape, let
the photographer's hooded camera pass,
the coroner in his lab coat, the DA
in her creased black pants.

Who thought
to bring these distracting flowers?
Who pushed
out the screen and broke the lock?
Who let him in?
Who cut the phone cord, the throat,
the wrist, the cake
on a plate and sat down and ate
only half?

What good is my life if I can't read the clues,
my mind the glue and each puzzle piece
chewed by the long-gone dog who raced
through the door, ran through our legs
and knocked over the vase,
hurtled down the alley and into the street?

What are we but meat, flesh
and the billion veins to be bled?
Why do we die this way, our jaws
open, our eyes bulging, as if there
were something to see or say?
Though today the flowers speak to me,
they way they sprawl in the streaked light,
their velvet lips and lids opening as I watch,
as if they wanted to go on living, climb
my pant legs, my wrinkled shirt, reach up
past my throat and curl over my mouth,
my eyes. Bury me in bloom.

BOB DYLAN

"Father of minutes, Father of days . . ."

I was born without a father, born again
without another. I searched the grassy
corridors of childhood, calling his name.
Only the birds called back, then returned
to ordering their feathers, dipping their beaks
in muddy gutter water. If I kill an ant
I kill it dead. I don't want anything to suffer.
Once I brushed a stinging column of them
from my pants. I got down on my knees,
watched how one, without a leg, limped
in circles, sent two front legs out to stroke
a crooked antenna, a gesture
that looked to me like prayer. I knew
it wasn't true. I knew there was no mercy
but me. So I went on with my empty plate,
like everyone else, calling, calling.
That's what the old man is doing now,
sleeping under a bare tree in the park,
his sack of clothes beneath his matted head.
He's twitching in dream. One hand clutching
the bald earth, the other waving me down.

MINE OWN PHIL LEVINE

after W. S. Merwin

What he told me, I will tell you
There was a war on
It seemed we had lived through
Too many to name, to number

There was no arrogance about him
No vanity, only the strong backs
Of his words pressed against
The tonnage of a page

His suggestion to me was that hard work
Was the order of each day
When I asked again, he said it again,
pointing it out twice

His Muse, if he had one, was a window
Filled with a brick wall, the left-hand corner
Of his mind, a hand lined with grease
And sweat: literal things

Before I knew him, I was unknown
I drank deeply from his knowledge
A cup he gave me again and again
Filled with water, clear river water

He was never old, and never grew older
Though the days passed and the poems
Marched forth and they were his words
Only, no others were needed

He advised me to wait, to hold true
To my vision, to speak in my own voice
To say the thing straight out
There was the whole day about him

The greatest thing, he said, was presence
To be yourself in your own time, to stand up
That poetry was precision, raw precision
Truth and compassion: genius

I had hardly begun. I asked, How did you begin
He said, I began in a tree, in Lucerne
In a machine shop, in an open field
Start anywhere

He said If you don't write, it won't
Get written. No tricks. No magic
About it. He gave me his gold pen
He said What's mine is yours.

THE BEATLES

I never really understood why The Beatles
broke up, the whole
Yoko Ono thing seemed an excuse
for something deeper.
Sure, she was an irritation
with her helium screech, her skimpy
leatherette skirts, those tinted ovoid glasses
eclipsing half her face.

    But come on, *Hey Jude*
was putting caviar on the table, not to mention
those glittering lines of cocaine. Beatle music
was paying for moats dug out with a fleet
of backhoes circling the stadium-sized perimeters
of four manicured estates. *Why Don't We
Do It In the Road* was backing up traffic
around the amphitheaters of the industrial world.
Yoko's avant-garde art projects and op-art
outfits were nothing against the shiploads of lucre
I'm Fixing a Hole and *Here Comes the Sun*
were bringing in.

So why did they do it?
They had wives, kids, ex-wives, mortgages,
thoroughbreds and waist-coated butlers, lithe
young assistants power-lunching with publicists
in Paris, Rome. And they must have loved
one another almost as much as John
loved Yoko, brothers from the ghetto,
their shaggy heads touching
above the grand piano, their voices
straining toward perfect harmony.

Maybe they arrived
at a place where nothing seemed real. A field
bigger than love or greed or jealousy.
An open space
where nothing is enough.

FOURTH OF JULY

The neighborhood cringes behind windows
washed in magnesium light, streamers fizzling
above the shingled rooftop of the apartments
across the street where teenaged boys
with mannish arms throw cherry bombs,
bottle rockets, wings and spinners, snappers,
chasers, fiery cryolite wheels onto the avenue.
Paint flakes off the flammable houses
and onto brave square plots of white grass.
Rain-deprived vines sucker the shutters.
Backyard dogs tear at the dirt, cats
run flat out, their tails straight up.
What's liberty to the checkout girl
selling smokes and nuts, greenbacks
turning her fingers to grease? The boys
insist on pursuing happiness, their birthright:
a box of matches, crackers on strings,
sparklers, fountains, missiles, repeating shells,
Roman candles, Brazilian barrages.
We peek through blind slats to where they stand
around a manhole cover, the gold foam
of Corona bottles breaking at their feet,
young up-turned faces lit by large caliber
multi-shot aerials. We suffer each concussion,

the sulfur rush that smells like fear, each dizzy,
orgiastic display that says we love this country,
democracy, the right to a speedy trial. We're afraid
to complain, to cross the spent red casings
melted on asphalt in the morning's stunned
aftermath, to knock hard on any door, and find them
draped like dead men over the couches, the floor,
hands clasped behind their heads prison style,
shoulders tattooed, dreaming the dreams of free men
in summer, shirts off, holes in their jeans.

TWO

THE SECRET OF BACKS

Heels of the shoes worn down, each
in its own way, sending signals to the spine.

The back of the knee as it folds and unfolds.
In winter the creases of American-made jeans:
blue denim seams worried to white threads.

And in summer, in spring, beneath the hems
of skirts, Bermudas, old bathing suit elastic,
the pleating and un-pleating of parchment skin.

And the dear, dear rears. Such variety! Such
choice in how to cover or reveal: belts looped high
or slung so low you can't help but think of plumbers.

And the small of the back: dimpled or taut, spiny or not,
tattooed, butterflied, rosed, winged, whorled. Maybe
still pink from the needle and ink. And shoulders,

broad or rolled, poking through braids, dreads, frothy
waterfalls of uncut hair, exposed to rain, snow, white
stars of dandruff, unbrushed flecks on a blue-black coat.

And the spiral near the top of the head—
peek of scalp, exquisite galaxy—as if the first breach
swirled each filament away from that startled center.

Ah, but the best are the bald or neatly shorn, revealing
the flanged, sun-flared, flamboyant backs of ears: secret
as the undersides of leaves, the flipside of flower petals.

And oh, the *oh my* nape of the neck. The up-swept *oh my*
nape of the neck. I could walk behind anyone and fall in love.

Don't stop. Don't turn around.

FOSTER CHILD

I didn't know our father owned a gun
until the day Jimmy came hopping into the garage
on one foot, his black high-top
filled with blood. I don't remember much—
how the cops got called, where they took him,
how long he got put on restriction—all I saw
was the fine red stream slipping
down his shoe lace, swirling into the rainbow oil
in the big silver pan my father drove the car over
to let it tick off to sleep. And later,
the cast, blind-white and hard,
the dirty worms of his toes, a bald knee
peeking out over the ragged lip.
He was already old when our mom took him in.
Wild, she said, her job to tame him. Love,
she told us, was all it took. Young still
when he left us to live at the Boy's Home,
away from matches and cans of gasoline,
kitchen knives and dirty magazines, stolen cigarettes
and baggies of pot, our mother's sweaty beers.
Maybe he lived with us a year, long enough
to start calling him brother, to recognize
the sound of his bike coming up the driveway,
our playing cards clothes-pinned to the wheel frame,

braking hard to send out a wing of gravel
with the slide of his back tire. Long enough
to see the cast removed, the wound healed over,
the scar deep and perfectly round, exactly the size
of the tip of my little finger, size of the bullet
we searched for and never found.

LOST IN COSTCO

Our mother wandered the aisles in the city
of canned goods and 30-lb. sacks
of dog food, mountains of sweat pants
and cheap jeans, open bins of discounted CDs.
She rested for a moment on the edge
of a bed in the furniture section,
trying to remember if it was time to sleep,
then headed off to garden supplies
where she stared at the glazed pots, missing
her roses, the ones she planted
outside the house she had to sell with the tree
she wanted to be buried under, her ashes
sealed in a See's Candy tin. We found her
on a piano bench, her purse beside her
like a canvas familiar, her fingers
running over the keys, playing the songs
she loved, taking requests from the crowd
gathered under the buzzing fluorescent lights.
Faking it, picking out the tunes, striking
a chord like she'd do when we were young
and she'd say sing it to me and we'd hum
a few bars: pop songs and Top 40 hits,
TV theme songs or chewing gum jingles,
our high, sweet voices giving her
so little to go on.

THE RISING

The pregnant mare at rest in the field
the moment we drove by decided
to stand up, rolled her massive body
sideways over the pasture grass,
gathered her latticed spine, curved ribs
between the hanging pots of flesh,
haunches straining, knee bones bent
on the bent grass cleaved
astride the earth she pushed against
to lift the brindled breast, the architecture
of the neck, the anvil head, her burred mane
tossing flames as her forelegs unlatched in air
while her back legs, buried beneath her belly,
set each horny hoof in opposition
to the earth, a counterweight concentrated there,
and by a willful rump and switch of tail hauled up,
flank and fetlock, her beastly burden, seized
and rolled and wrenched and winched the wave
of her body, the grand totality of herself,
to stand upright in the depth of that field.
The heaviness of gravity upon her.
The strength of the mother.

SECOND CHANCES

What are the chances a raindrop
from last night's storm caught
in the upturned cup of an autumn leaf
will fall from this tree I pass under
and land on the tip of my lit cigarette,
snuffing it out? What are the chances
my niece will hit bottom before Christmas,
a drop we all long for, and quit heroin?
What are the chances of being hit
by a bus, a truck, a hell-bound train
or inheriting the gene for cancer,
addiction? What good are statistics
on a morning like this? What good
is my niece to anyone but herself?
What are the chances any of you
are reading this poem?
                                    Dear men,
whom I have not met,
when you meet her on the street
wearing the wounds that won't heal
and she offers you the only thing
she has left, what are the chances
you'll take pity on her fallen body?

MIDDLE NAME

The photograph is black and white
and it's snowing, so I don't know the color
of her hair, her dress, the blanket
I'm wrapped in—2 days old—a close-up,
her eyes cast down, my mother's
best friend, my namesake Louise,
the third woman to hold me, the first
being an anonymous nurse, probably
older than my young mother
in the month of January, in the year
1952, probably dead now, her bones
naked beneath the ground. And Louise,
who was she, the woman who held
the small, warm engine of my body,
the one my mother loved enough
to give me her name, to find a camera
and take this photograph, Louise,
keeper of my mother's secrets and dreams,
her arm arced beneath me, her fingers
pinching the wool brim of my cap
to shield my eyes from the snow, the cold,
holding me so tight and close
she could be mistaken for a mother,
this friend who disappeared into

the past, whose scent I breathed in,
whose breast I turned to, the names
of saints carved into the stone arch
of the church behind her, snow
on the roof, the sky white, her scarf
might be yellow, it might be blue.

FOG

The first of us must have looked up at the night agog,
so many stars, so much light falling down, the bugs
back then big as fists, so many rivers and ponds clogged
with fish we skewered them on sticks, made a fire, bred dogs
from wolves to keep us warm, safe, pines wrapped in fog
or morning mist, the sheep braying beside us, groggy,
their bellies filled with wet grass, the feral pigs become hogs
in a pen, cloven hooves slathered in mud. We built jagged
fences to keep what we didn't want out, what we did, in, logs
were dragged through a field by horses, a house rose, mugs
placed on a shelf, a table set with plates. Then the nagging
began: Who left the feedbag in the rain? Who forgot to plug
the hole with a rag? The children grew, little quagmires
we sank into. We fed them, scrubbed them, raised them, rang
a bell for supper, school, for the one who died, the soggy
earth taking her back, the others running unaware, tagging
each other in the dusk, calling out numbers. But still the vague
unrest in the dark looking up at the moon, the old dog wagging
his tick-laden tail, barking for no reason they could tell, zagging
off like an uncle, drunk on busthead whiskey, back into the trees.

ANTILAMENTATION

Regret nothing. Not the cruel novels you read
to the end just to find out who killed the cook, not
the insipid movies that made you cry in the dark,
in spite of your intelligence, your sophistication, not
the lover you left quivering in a hotel parking lot,
the one you beat to the punch line, the door or the one
who left you in your red dress and shoes, the ones
that crimped your toes, don't regret those.
Not the nights you called god names and cursed
your mother, sunk like a dog in the living room couch,
chewing your nails and crushed by loneliness.
You were meant to inhale those smoky nights
over a bottle of flat beer, to sweep stuck onion rings
across the dirty restaurant floor, to wear the frayed
coat with its loose buttons, its pockets full of struck matches.
You've walked those streets a thousand times and still
you end up here. Regret none of it, not one
of the wasted days you wanted to know nothing,
when the lights from the carnival rides
were the only stars you believed in, loving them
for their uselessness, not wanting to be saved.

You've traveled this far on the back of every mistake,
ridden in dark-eyed and morose but calm as a house
after the TV set has been pitched out the window.
Harmless as a broken ax. Emptied of expectation.
Relax. Don't bother remembering any of it. Let's stop here,
under the lit sign on the corner, and watch all the people walk by.

CHER

I wanted to be Cher, tall
as a glass of iced tea,
her bony shoulders draped
with a curtain of dark hair
that plunged straight down,
the cut tips brushing
her nonexistent butt.
I wanted to wear a lantern
for a hat, a cabbage, a piñata
and walk in thigh-high boots
with six-inch heels that buttoned
up the back. I wanted her
rouged cheek bones and her
throaty panache, her voice
of gravel and clover, the hokum
of her clothes: black fishnet
and pink pom-poms, frilled
halter tops, fringed bells
and her thin strip of waist
with the bullet-hole navel.
Cher standing with her skinny arm
slung around Sonny's thick neck,
posing in front of the Eiffel Tower,
The Leaning Tower of Pisa,

The Great Wall of China,
The Crumbling Pyramids, smiling
for the camera with her crooked
teeth, hit-and-miss beauty, the sun
bouncing off the bump on her nose.
Give me back the old Cher,
the gangly, imperfect girl
before the shaving knife
took her, before they shoved
pillows in her tits, injected
the lumpy gel into her lips.
Take me back to the woman
I wanted to be, stalwart
and silly, smart as her lion
tamer's whip, my body a torch
stretched the length of the polished
piano, legs bent at the knee, hair
cascading down over Sonny's blunt
fingers as he pummeled the keys,
singing in a sloppy alto
the oldest, saddest songs.

THE MYSTERIOUS HUMAN HEART
IN NEW YORK

Streetwise but foolish, the heart
knows what's good for it but goes
for the dark bar, the beer before noon,
the doughy pretzel hot and salty, tied up
in a Gordian knot. It takes a walk
through Tompkins Square where
the homeless sleep it off on stone benches,
one shrouded body to each gritty sarcophagus.
The streets fill with taxis and trucks,
pinstripes and briefcases, and the subways
spark and sway underground. The sun
is snagged on the Empire State, performing
its one-note song, the citizens below
dragging their shadows down the sidewalk
like sidekicks, spitting into the gutter
as if on cue, as if in a musical,
as if there's no association between the trash
flapping against the chain link and the girl
with her skirt up in the alley. When the traffic
jams on 110th—a local pain, a family affair—
the Starbucks junkie leans against the glass
and laughs into his hand, a cabbie
sits on his hood and smokes, cops
on skates weave through the exhaust,

billy club blunts bumping against their
dark blue thighs. Everyone's on a cell phone,
the air a-buzz with yammer and electricity
as the heart of the city pounds like a man
caught in the crosswalk holding his shoulder,
going down on one knee, then blundering
into Central Park to lean over the addled bridge,
the sooty swans floating under him, grown fat
on cheap white bread. Oh heart, with your
empty pockets and your hat on backwards,
stop looking at yourself in the placid waters.
Someone is sneaking up behind you
in an overcoat lined with watches,
and someone else is holding a cardboard sign
that says: The End Is Here.

DOG MOON

The old dog next door won't stop barking
at the moon. My neighbor is keeping a log:
what time, how long, whether howling is involved.
I know she's awake as I am, robe askew,
calling animal control while I drink dark tea
and stare out my window at the voodoo moon,
throwing beads of light into the arms
of the bare-chested trees. Who can blame him
when the moon is as big as a kitchen clock
and ticking like a time bomb? The bright full moon
with its beryl core and striated face, its plasma umbra,
pouring borrowed light into every abyss on earth,
turning the rivers silver, plowing the mountains'
shadows across grasslands and deserts, towns
riddled with mineshafts, oil rigs and mills,
yellow tractors asleep in the untilled fields.
The what-were-they-like moon staring down
on rain-pocked gravestones, worming its way
into gopher holes, setting barbed wire fences ablaze.
Who wouldn't love this old-tooth moon,
this toilet-paper moon? This feral, flea-bitten moon
is that dog's moon, too. Certain-of-nothing moon, bone
he can't wait to sink his teeth into. Radio moon,
the white dial tuned to static. Panic moon,

pulling clouds like blankets over its baby face.
Moon a portrait hung from a nail
in the starred hallway of the past.
Full moon that won't last.
I can hear that dog clawing at the fence.
Moon a manhole cover sunk in the boulevard
of night, monocle on a chain, well of light,
a frozen pond lifted and thrown like a discus
onto the sky. I scratch my skull, look down
into my stained empty cup. That dog
has one blind eye, the other one's looking up.

TO KISS FRANK . . .

make out with him a bit, this
is what my friend would like to do
oh these too many dead summers later,
and as much as I want to stroll with her
into the poet's hazy fancy
all I can see is O'Hara's long-gone lips
fallen free of the bone, slumbering
beneath the grainy soil.
I can hear Frank's dry voice
combing the air for song, but what I see
is his skeleton entombed in dust, wrapped
in his dapper suit, his razzle-dazzle sunglasses.
She sees him alive, ambling
down a sidewalk, all of New York
clambering into the sky behind him,
cuff links winking, his dear friends waving,
calling him by name like they do in the city:
800,000 people and you step outside for a smoke
and see someone you know.
That's how it is with death.
Those you love come at you like lightning,
crackle for an instant—so kissable—
and then lips and all, they're gone.

DARK CHARMS

Eventually the future shows up everywhere:
those burly summers and unslept nights in deep
lines and dark splotches, thinning skin.
Here's the corner store grown to a condo,
the bike reduced to one spinning wheel,
the ghost of a dog that used to be, her trail
no longer trodden, just a dip in the weeds.
The clear water we drank as thirsty children
still runs through our veins. Stars we saw then
we still see now, only fewer, dimmer, less often.
The old tunes play and continue to move us
in spite of our learning, the wraith of romance,
lost innocence, literature, the death of the poets.
We continue to speak, if only in whispers,
to something inside us that longs to be named.
We name it the past and drag it behind us,
bag like a lung filled with shadow and song,
dreams of running, the keys to lost names.

GOLD

Color of JCPenney's jewelry, trinket
in a Cracker Jack box, color of roadside
weeds, candy wrapper in a gutter. Color

of streamers tied to the handlebars
of a rusty bike, color of rust on the bike's
dented fender. Color of food stamps
and welfare checks, dirt swept into
the long hole of the missing board
on the back porch, the untended sore,
phlegm in the hotel toilet bowl. Color

of mold in the broken refrigerator, lightbulb
hung over the dog-shredded screen,
color of curtainless kitchen windows
throbbing through the dark, underwear
stains, old bandages, knees of worn jeans,
filters of generic cigarettes, brand X
bottles of beer, lighter flints, match heads,
dry leaves. Color

of blocks of cheese and government butter,
rolled oats, crust of white bread, bacon fat,
two fingers of oil shivering in the pan,
chicken wings dragged through cornmeal,
the three-legged cat, two hairs left
on the naked doll's bald head, the spikes
in the iris of her rolling eye, the bottoms
of unwashed feet, seals on divorce papers,
notices of default, ancient coat hangers, bingo
chips, the pawned topaz ring, lottery tickets,
mustard on a cracker, sulfur, factory lights
at night, hills of sawdust and shallow pans
of brake fluid, bees seething in a dead tree knot,
tinder in a box, pennies in a jar, coffee-stained
teeth, a busted piano's ivory keys, bed bugs, fleas,
algae scum simmering on a pond, the carp
floating beneath. Color

of the crane and chain of the wrecking ball
stranded in sun glare, the loud bell of the sun,
the clock-ticking stars, shade in the bathroom
stuck halfway down, rag rugs, lye soap,
nicotine slick in the grooves of kitchen ashtrays,
the worn handles of soup ladles, tin roses
painted on the stillborn baby's shoebox cradle,
brass tip of the veteran's cane, Gold Bond powder
that eats sweat from the creases, A and D ointment,
Listerine, dirt roads, fool's gold, litter of kittens
in the corn crib, tobacco spit, strip of light
under the closed door. Color

of unshaven stubble along the scar on a man's
cheek, floor wax on a woman's knees, bouillon
cubes in foil, the backs of flies in spiderwebs,
fishing line at sunset, honey in a bucket, dead
clover, color

of the edges of bargain basement books
dropped in the bin, dust rising in motes
onto the long tables in the public library
where the homeless come to sit in rows,
heads fallen on their folded arms
like good school children dreaming of sleep.

MOTHER'S DAY

I passed through the narrow hills
of my mother's hips one cold morning
and never looked back, until now, clipping
her tough toenails, sitting on the bed's edge
combing out the tuft of hair at the crown
where it ratted up while she slept, her thumbs
locked into her fists, a gesture as old
as she is, her blanched knees fallen together
beneath a blue nightgown. The stroke

took whole pages of words, random years
torn from the calendar, the names of roses
leaning over her driveway: Cadenza,
Great Western, American Beauty. She can't
think, can't drink her morning tea, do her
crossword puzzle in ink. She's afraid
of everything, the sound of the front door
opening, light falling through the blinds—
pulls her legs up so the bright bars
won't touch her feet. I help her
with the buttons on her sweater. She looks
hard at me and says the word sleeve.
Exactly, I tell her and her face relaxes
for the first time in days. I lie down

next to her on the flowered sheets and tell her
a story about the day she was born, head
first into a hard world: the Great Depression,
shanties, Hoovervilles, railroads and unions.
I tell her about Amelia Earhart and she asks

Air? and points to the ceiling. Asks Heart?
and points to her chest. Yes, I say. I sing
Cole Porter songs, *Brother, Can You Spare
a Dime?* When I recite lines from *Gone
with the Wind* she sits up and says Potatoes!
and I say, Right again. I read her Sandburg,
some Frost, and she closes her eyes. I say yes,
yes, and tuck her in. It's summer. She's tired.
No one knows where she's been.

EMILY SAID

Emily said she heard a fly buzz
when she died, heard it whizz
over her head, troubling her frizzed
hair. What will I hear? Showbiz
tunes on the radio, the megahertz
fuzz when the station picks up Yaz,
not the Hall-of-Famer or the Pez
of contraceptives, but the jazzy
flash-in-the-pan '80's techo-pop star, peach fuzz
on her rouged cheeks singing *Pal-ease*
Don't Go through a kazoo. Will my old love spritz
the air with the perfume of old roses,
buy me the white satin Mercedes-Benz
of pillows, string a rainbow blitz
of crystals in the window—quartz, topaz—
or will I die wheezing, listening to a quiz
show: What year is this? Who was the 44th Prez
of the United States? Where is the Suez
Canal? Are you too hot? Cold? Freezing?

OVER THE HEDGE

We labor in the backyard, weeding,
pulling stones like tumors up
from the hardened clay, lumpy
ogre-piles of rock-clod-weed:
scare-crowish. Back to bent back,
we are tin-foil and matchstick, stooped
over our rakes like Van Gogh's long dead
Haymakers, though maybe happier
in our work, work that brings forth
little more than a few ratty tomatoes,
knobby volunteer potatoes, the odd
renegade squash. We leave in the wild
carrots and hollow onion stalks, deadhead
the gangly rogue rose we've grown to love
like a headstrong adolescent boy.
It's mostly exercise for the quickly aging here:
fresh air, a loss of self-consciousness, to be
without thought among the reedy weeds,
brushing gnats from our eyes, pollen-
fingered, followed by bursts of orgiastic sneezing
stopping us in our tracks.
We tug up feeder root saplings knowing
in some distant way that without us
this garden will, in a few untended years,

become a forest of oak and ash,
the lilac, thriving now, will become stunted,
shriveled, curled up like an old woman
in the deadly hemlock shade. This patch
of grass we stand in, freshly mown,
will dwindle to a few scruffy tufts,
and the porch with its new coat
of off-white paint is really nothing more
than a future ladder for the un-removable
morning glory. And the ivy will crawl down
from its banks in a slow green wave
to cover the driveway's broken shore,
then climb our shingled house, growing over
the windows we washed just last week,
one inside, one out, rags in our hands,
working circles in tandem, making
faces at each other through the glass.

WHO NEEDS US?

The quiet, the bitter, the bereaved,
the going forth of us, the coming home,
the drag and pull of us, the tome and teem
and tensile greed of us, the opening
and closing of us, our eyes, in sleep,
our crematorium dreams?

The brush of us one against another,
the crumple on the couch of us,
the spring in our step, the sequestered dance
in front of the cracked mirrors of us,
our savage suffering, our wobbly ladders
of despair, the drenched seaweed-green
of our tipped wineglass hearts, our wheels
and guitars, white spider bites blooming
on our many-colored skins, the din
of our nerves, our pearl onion toes
and orangey fingers, our effigies
and empty bellies, our plazas
of ache and despair, our dusky faces
round as dinner plates, our bald pates,
our doubt, our clout, our bold mistakes?

Who needs the footprints of us,
the glimpse of us in a corridor of stars,
who sees the globes of our breath
before us in winter, the angels
we make in the stiff snow,
the hack and ice of us, the glide
and gleam and busted puzzle of us,
the myth and math of us,
the blue bruise and excuse of us,
who will know the magnified
magnificence of us, could there be
too many of us, the clutch and strum
and feral singing of us, the hush of us,
who will hear the whisker of silence
we will leave in our wake?

FALL

I'm tired of stories about the body,
how important it is, how unimportant,
how you're either a body
hauling a wrinkled brain around
or a brain trailing a stunned sheen
of flesh. Or those other questions
like Would you rather love or be loved?
If you could come back as the opposite sex,
what would you do first? As if. As if.
Yes the body is lonely, especially at twilight.
Yes Baptists would rather you not have a body at all,
especially not breasts, suspended in their hooked bras
like loose prayers, like ticking bombs, like two
Hallelujahs, the choir frozen in their onyx gowns
like a row of flashy Cadillacs, their plush upholstery
hidden behind tinted windows, Jesus swinging
from the rearview mirror by a chain.
And certainly not the body in the autumn
of its life, humming along in a wheelchair,
legs withered beneath the metallic shine
of thinning skin. No one wants to let
that body in. Especially not the breasts again,

your mother's are strangers to you now, your sister's
were always bigger and clung to her blouse,
your lover's breasts, deep under the ground,
you weep beside the little mounds of earth
lightly shoveled over them.

ROOTS

The pine clings to the cliff side, angles
seaward above the waves, its exposed roots
attended by flowering weeds. Those fingers
will someday lose their grip, this is clear
to any one of us, and I believe the tree, too,
knows its long life will be cut short and
doesn't care. Why would it? Who among us
wouldn't give a year or more to lean against
the wind and gaze down into the void? And
doesn't this dark desire to fall exist in every heart?
I remember my first fast car ride at midnight,
stoplights streaking by, rings of fire
on that beach where I first dipped my tongue
into the wet salty cave of the beloved's mouth,
the fury with which I took the other's flesh inside me,
the hard pits of the first fruit I chewed and sucked.
Now, in my calm backyard, I watch clouds
tear themselves apart around the stars,
listen to the possum's claws rake and rasp
against the trashcan's metal sides, inhale
the blossoming cherry growing up over
the shed's flat roof. She drops her petals there
to make a carpet of snow. Even this far from
the ocean she knows what is possible, yet

is content to stand here, burrowing
into the clay earth, feeder roots worming
through hair-thin holes in the rusted
underground pipes. Even so,
her lithe arms sway in the night breeze
and a few bright petals settle
onto the black pond. They float only a moment
before the moon-colored carp finds them
with his hairy ancient lips, and one by one,
carries them down.

ACKNOWLEDGMENTS

The Alaska Quarterly Review, The American Poetry Review, The Columbia Poetry Review, The Cortland Review, Crab Creek Review, CRATE, Cutthroat, diode, Fight These Bastards, Grist, High Desert Journal, Line Break, MiPOesis, The National Poetry Review, The Normal School, Oregon Literary Review, Orion Magazine, The Pedestal Magazine, Poetrybay, PROJECT Silence, Red Wheelbarrow, River Styx, The Seattle Review, Tin House, TriQuarterly Review, Valpariso Poetry Review, Willow Springs

"Dark Charms" was chosen for Best of the Net by Sundress Press and was reprinted in the Alhambra Poetry Calendar

"Over the Hedge" and "Dog Moon" were reprinted on *Verse Daily*

"Cher" was reprinted in *Third Rail: The Poetry of Rock and Roll* (MTV Books), *Writing the Life Poetic: An Invitation to Read and Write Poetry*, ed. Sage Cohen, 2009 and the Alhambra Poetry Calendar

"Juneau" was reprinted in *New Labor Forum: A Journal of Ideas, Analysis, and Debate*

"The Rising" was published in *Cadence of Hooves: A Celebration of Horses*

"Superman," "Cher," "The Beatles," "Late Night TV," and "Bakersfield" appeared in *Superman: The Chapbook* (Red Dragonfly Press, 2008)

"Dark Charms," "Dog Moon," "Emily Said," "Fog," "Men," "The Mysterious Human Heart in New York," and "Gold" appeared in *Dark Charms* (Red Dragonfly Press, 2009)

"Cher" is for Lory "Armo" Bedikian

"Dark Charms" is for Maxine Scates, Bill Cadbury, and Stella

"Bob Dylan" is for Nick Flynn

"Foster Child" is for Jimmy Daugneault

"Juneau" is for Paul and Susie

"Learning to Drive" is for Bill Byas

"Roots" is for Frank X. Gaspar

"Second Chances" is for Monica

"The Beatles" is for Joel Rosen

"The Mysterious Human Heart in New York" is for Dave Grubin

"To Kiss Frank . . ." is for Michelle Bitting

"Staff Sgt. Metz" is for Doug Anderson and Brian Turner

"Dog Moon" is for Amy Cruz

Thanks to all named above as well as Joseph Millar, Nancy Hechinger, Philip Levine, Sharon Olds, Jill Bialosky, and my assistant, Michelle Bitting, and to my delightful and supportive colleagues at NCSU and Pacific University's Low Residency MFA Program. Thanks again and again to Joel Rosen, Tristem, and the boys, and to Ellen Bass and Janet Bryer for their summer sanctuary in Santa Cruz.

Gratitude to The Virginia Center for the Creative Arts for residencies that allowed me to complete this work, to *Poetry Daily* and *Verse Daily,* which gave some of these poems a second life, and to Scott King at Red Dragonfly Press.

In memory of Carol Houck Smith, Lucille Clifton, Ai, and Deborah Digges.

NOTES

"Bob Dylan"—The epigraph is a line from Bob Dylan's song *Father of Night*.

"Fog," "Emily Said," and "Men" all follow a similar form wherein the last word of each line ends in the same sound.

Into Great Silence (Die Große Stille) is a documentary film directed by Philip Gröning that was first released in 2005. It is an intimate portrayal of the everyday lives of monks of the Grande Chartreuse, high in a remote corner of the French Alps. The film was made sixteen years after the director first requested permission to make it. He lived at the monastery for six months, and filmed alone, behind the walls no "outsider" had ever before been allowed to enter.

"Mine Own Phil Levine" is closely patterned after W. S. Merwin's poem "Berryman" and the title is taken from Philip Levine's essay titled "Mine Own John Berryman," which in turn is based on the Thomas Wyatt poem, "Mine Own John Poins."